My Haggadah Journal

A GUIDED JOURNEY TO HEAL, GROW, AND THRIVE

BY NECHAMA DINA WASSERMAN LABER
ART BY CHANA LABER

My Haggadah Journal
A Guided Journey to Heal, Grow, and Thrive

ISBN 978-0-9841624-8-2

Second Edition - Nissan 5782 / April 2022

Copyright © 2022 by JGU Press

A project of Jewish Girls Unite
5 Mannix Rd
East Greenbush, NY 12061
www.JewishGirlsUnite.com

ALL RIGHTS RESERVED
No part of this book may be reproduced in any form without written permission from the copyright holder.

Layout by Carasmatic Design - www.carasmaticdesign.com

Printed in the USA

Dedicated to

MICKI & NORMAN MASSRY
& their beloved children
JULIE & JIM, MURRAY & MALLORY, LAURIE & KEN
& their families.

&

LINDA & ORY SCHWARTZ
& their beloved children
MEIRAH, SIVAN, LIELLE & YOSEF

For their selfless & generous support that is empowering women & girls worldwide!

May you & all of Klal Yisroel be blessed with health, wealth & nachas!

With Love & Appreciation
Nechama Laber &
The Jewish Girls Unite Global Family

DEAR READER,

We are thrilled to present to you the *My Haggadah Journal* as a gift to enrich your Pesach. It is based on the teachings of the Lubavitcher Rebbe and personal-growth tools connected to the Haggadah text. It is not a complete Haggadah, but rather highlights selections to guide your individual journey from *"slavery to freedom; sorrow to joy; mourning to celebration; darkness to great light; and servitude to redemption"* (*Haggadah*). Please enjoy this *Haggadah Journal* to discover **YOUR** story and navigate out of a personal Egypt.

Our Sages say that our journey to redemption will be similar to the Exodus from Egypt. The Hebrew name for Egypt, Mitzrayim, also means "limitation." This alludes to the idea that Pesach, the Season of Our Freedom, is an auspicious time to challenge some of our limiting beliefs and free ourselves from our psychological and spiritual limitations. Pesach takes place at the beginning of spring, when new blossoms begin to sprout. It symbolizes the soul within yearning to grow and break through its personal Egypt.

The Talmud records that only twenty percent of the Jewish people departed Egypt and eighty percent stayed behind because they were assimilated and immersed in Egyptian society. The Haggadah tells the story of our ancestors who had the courage and foresight to leave.

We may think that it is difficult to heal, grow and thrive. We may feel that we don't have the strength and stamina to break out of our boundaries. The Haggadah reminds us that we are part of the group that made it out of Egypt, and we received the ability from our ancestors to liberate ourselves with help from Hashem.

The Talmud (*Pesachim 116b*) teaches, "In every generation, one must see oneself as if one has personally gone out of Egypt." The Holy One, blessed be He, not only redeemed our ancestors, but He also redeemed us with them. As it says: "He brought us out from there in order to bring and give us the land which He had promised to our ancestors" (*Devarim, 6:23*).

The word *Haggadah* means "to tell." It is a Torah commandment to tell the story of our ancestors, in order to preserve the lessons for generations. The Seder is a perfect opportunity to fortify our link to the past, our strength in the present, and our hope for the future.

Our JGU mission is to empower women and girls to internalize the wisdom of Torah as the guide for life. We are here for you and committed to increasing the light through online programs and resources that inspire and uplift girls and women worldwide. Sign up for JGU online programs and Grow Connection Circles at JewishGirlsUnite.com, retreats at GreenbushRetreat.com, or book a coaching session with Nechama Laber at 518.727.9581.

May we be blessed with the light of the Ultimate Redemption, and merit to spend Pesach together, THIS YEAR IN JERUSALEM!

Wishing you and your loved ones a kosher and joyous Pesach!

With blessings,

The JGU Press & The Connection Project Team

Acknowledgments

We were inspired to create this *Haggadah Journal* during the Covid lockdown in March 2020. When our Pesach retreat guests canceled, we found ourselves with extra time to develop this journal. My daughter Chana and assistant Tzipporah joined the team as the artist and editor. We offered online workshops focused on the deeper spiritual meaning of the Haggadah and how it is a guide to heal, grow and thrive. We are grateful to all our participants who joined us on this journey to freedom.

During summer 2019, the JGU Press published my memoir, *Finding Song in Sorrow* (available on Amazon.com). This endeavor clearly showed me how sharing my story provides hope and healing to others facing challenges. I am forever grateful to Micki and Norman Massry for supporting Jewish girls worldwide with their love and generosity. They made it possible to publish my book and establish our Jewish Greenbush Retreat campus to create a beautiful space for others to discover their story of hope and healing.

I am grateful to Hashem for my life and my mission; and to the Lubavitcher Rebbe for his guidance and wisdom that feeds my soul every day.

I am grateful to my father, a beloved educator, Rabbi Azriel Wasserman O"BM, who planted the seeds in me to grow my passion for Jewish education; my mother, Daniella Wasserman Katzenberg, who raised me in a beautiful home filled with the light of Torah; and Daddy Katzenberg, a Chazan, who adds joy and song to every Holiday celebration. Thank you to my supportive husband, Rabbi Avraham Laber, and my eleven children, K"H, for giving me the space to work on these projects.

With heartfelt appreciation to my mentors and supporters who continue to inspire and empower me to grow and expand our mission: Susan Axelrod, Malkah Blicburn, Nanette Brenner, Hannah Chakoff, Yocheved Daphna, Talia Edell, Marc and Judy Ehrlich, Rachel Federman, Shoshana

Fox, Julie Gniwisch, Mendy Gorodetsky, Chaya Sarah Gurewicz, Shlomie and Mirele Greenwald, Lori Hertzberg, Dr. Ed Jacobs, Rabbi Simon Jacobson, Racheli Jacks, Ellen Koplowitz, Yehudis Karbal, Chesky Kauftheil, Shaindel Leanse, Loren Lichtenstein, Micki Massry, Julie Massry Knox, Chana Zeldy Minkowitz, Rivka Malka Perlman and the Redemption School, Leah Namdar, Eli Nash, Chananya Rosenblum, Karen Sarto, Eda Schottenstein, Linda Schwartz, Rochi Shemtov, Dr. Daniel Schoenbach, Dobra Spinner, Rabbi Shais Taub, Ezzy and Chana Wasserman, Miriam Yerushalmi, and Nechama Dena Zweibel.

We are incredibly grateful to all of our many JGU students, campers and parents, Connection Circle participants, partners and supporters who launched JGU and The Connection Project (The-ConnectionProject.com) with the vital mission to help girls, women, and families heal, grow and thrive. Our unity is transforming thousands of lives every day.

Dear JGU Press team, with thanks to Hashem, we did it again! We look forward to creating more inspirational resources for our global community.

Thank you to my dear friend and artist, Chana Cotter for brainstorming this idea; my talented daughter Chana Laber for the beautiful illustrations and Ron Sohn and Chanie Chanin for the Miriam art; JGU editor Tzipporah Prottas who devoted countless hours to this project and Leah Caras for the beautiful design. Working together is a gift and helped me draw strength from our Haggadah in preparation for Pesach and the ultimate redemption.

With blessings,

Nechama Dina Wasserman Laber

JGU Global Director & Educator, Coach, Author

About the Author

Nechama Laber is the founder and global director of Jewish Girls Unite and The Connection Project, an experienced educator, Judaic consultant, Bat Mitzvah instructor, curriculum designer, certified life and connection coach, public speaker, and the author of *Finding Song in Sorrow*. She is co-director of Chabad of Southern Rensselaer County with her husband, Rabbi Avraham Laber, where they reside with their 11 children, K"H, and run the beloved Jewish Girls Retreat in summer and winter.

About the Artist

Chana Laber grew up on Shlichus in Upstate NY where she discovered the power of art to inspire. Her work focuses on powerful messages of Torah and Chassidus, exploring all mediums of art. She teaches art and Chassidus online and in person. Follow her journey on Instagram at @laberoflove.

Women & Girls

Shine your inner light!

Join online programs.

Get inspired & inspire others!

www.jewishgirlsunite.com

📷 @the-connectionproject

EVERY DETAIL IN THE STORY OF THE EXODUS ALSO SERVES AS A GUIDE IN OUR SPIRITUAL REDEMPTION FROM OUR PERSONAL EGYPT.

בְּכָל דוֹר וָדוֹר חַיָּב אָדָם לִרְאוֹת אֶת עַצְמוֹ כְּאִלּוּ הוּא יָצָא מִמִּצְרָיִם.

"In every generation one must see oneself as if one personally has gone out of Egypt."

(Talmud, Pesachim 116b)

Freedom — How do we define it? Is it to be untethered and unrestricted? The liberty to make our own choices? To live in an uncontrolled society? There's a freedom that transcends all parts of life.
A plant needs to be restricted and rooted in the ground to grow. Animals need to roam. A human being needs to keep his mind stimulated, to communicate and express with words.
For a plant to be ripped out of the ground, or an animal to be put in a cage, that is not freedom.
Our boundaries allow us to thrive.
Freedom is to be our authentic self
Fulfill our individual needs
Express our truth though our
unique boundaries of life

A Jew needs to be soul connected. Every Neshama has a mission and purpose. When the soul is expressed, that's when we are truly free.
-By Chana Laber

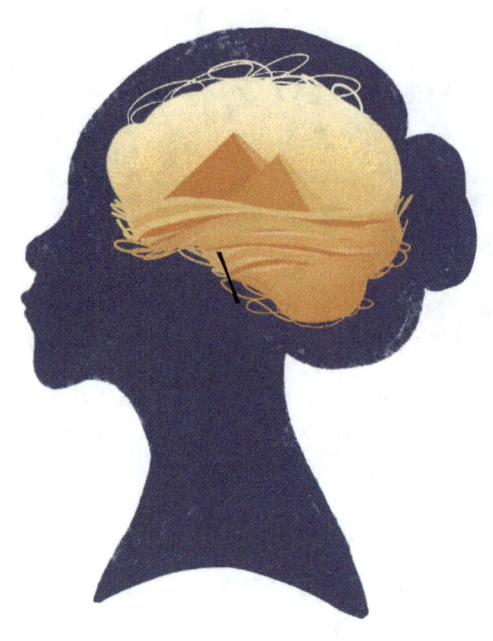

מִצְרַיִם Mitzrayim

mitz-RA-yim · Noun

1. Egypt (in Hebrew). It is a country located in the northeastern corner of Africa. Egypt's heartland, the Nile River valley and delta, was the home of one of the principal civilizations of the ancient Middle East and, like Mesopotamia farther east, was the site of one of the world's earliest urban and literate societies.

2. Limitation. According to the Zohar, the name is derived from "*meitzarim*," meaning 'from narrow straits.' These may include fear, anger, overwhelm, depression, laziness, apathy, arrogance, guilt, shame, unworthiness, insecurity, negative thoughts and habits that block and limit us from expressing and actualizing our true selves.

When Hashem took us out of *Mitzrayim*, He extricated us from Egypt, a place of constricted opportunities, tight control, and immorality. Pesach is when we focus inward to leave our mental, emotional, physical and spiritual Egypt that entraps our souls. We find purpose, take responsibility and experience true fulfillment, clarity, connection, love and joy.

What is your Egypt today?

This journey to freedom has baggage policies. In order to move forward, some things will have to be left behind.

Journey to Freedom

Racheli Jacks for JGR 2006 ©
Listen online at jewishgirlsunite.com/haggadah

Journey, Journey to freedom
Yatza, Yatza Mimitzrayim
In every generation, experience it again
Embarking on a journey within

Go out – rise above the challenge
See how - Hashem leads the way
When the fight gets tough
Just keep your goal in sight
A new step day by day

Chorus
Don't give up – keep on going
Faith and courage always showing
Help a friend – you're not alone
Traveling to Yisrael, our home

Travel – travel through the desert
Torah – leads us right along
All our needs provided, we'll journey to our land
United, hand in hand

Yes, I Believe

Rivka Leah Popack for Jewish Girls Unite ©
Listen online at jewishgirlsunite.com/haggadah

Did you hear the story told?
As each soul comes to this world
It answers the purpose of creation

Do you believe that it could be?
A single soul, like you or me
Could change the world and all we see forever

Plant a seed and watch it grow
Drop a stone, the ripples flow
Farther than you'd ever know

The sea is vast, the ocean's wide
But greater is your will inside
Geulah now, change the tide

Chorus
Yes, I believe like
the sunrise each day
Moshiach will come,
we'll bring him today
I believe like a flame burning bright
We'll shine through the darkness;
we'll light up the night
A moment the world is waiting for
Celebrate forevermore

Eternal light
Songs through the night
Dancing in sight

Women Unite
Reach within to find your art
The colors that define your heart
Each of us can paint our part

Inspire me; I'll inspire you
You'll hit a wall; I'll pull you through
Heart and soul in everything we do

A million beats of a million hearts
Where's your "Tof Beyadah"?
A new melody is about to start

Chorus

Vatikach Miriam Hanavia
Et Hatof Beyadah
Vataytzena Kol Hanoshim
B'Tupim Uvim'cholos
וַתִּקַּח מִרְיָם הַנְּבִיאָה אֶת־הַתֹּף בְּיָדָהּ
וַתֵּצֶאןָ כָל־הַנָּשִׁים בְּתֻפִּים וּבִמְחֹלֹת

Chorus

Eternal light
Songs through the night
Dancing in sight
Women Unite

I believe, with my tambourine,
Bizchus Nashim...

Seder in Egypt

THANK HASHEM IN ADVANCE FOR YOUR FREEDOM.

Pesach is different from other holidays because the Jews were commanded to have a Seder celebration, sacrifice a sheep and eat matzah and bitter herbs while still in Egypt. They earned redemption through their trust in Hashem by celebrating their Exodus in advance and with their courage to fulfill His will by slaughtering the deity of the Egyptians.

The first step towards redemption is to thank Hashem in advance and to discover the courage to follow and surrender to the will of Hashem.

Compose your thanks to Hashem in advance:

"Thank You, Hashem, for the strength and courage to break through my boundaries and limitations and for redeeming me from my personal Egypt."

Thank You…

ARE YOU READY WITH YOUR BELT, SHOES, AND STAFF?

The Jews were commanded to eat the Pesach offering "with your waist belted, your shoes on your feet and your staff in your hand" (*Shemos 12:11*).

This indicated the Jewish people's readiness to leave Egypt and their belief in their impending freedom.

There are three specific areas in which we strive to grow and accomplish: Within ourselves, our environment, and the greater world.

The way to achieve success in all these areas is hinted at in the above-quoted verse.

1. "With your WAIST belted."

The mid-section keeps the entire body upright and alludes to our upright conduct and effort to perform Mitzvos and refine our character.

2. "Your SHOES on your feet."

This refers to the action of stepping outside ourselves to enhance the lives of the people in our surroundings. Just like shoes protect the feet from the ground, we need extra protection from negative influences in our environment.

3. "STAFF in your hand."

This hints to the way in which one reaches out to the world. A walking stick enables us to reach places we cannot reach on our own. The Rambam teaches that every individual is obliged to say: 'The entire world was created for my sake." We have the responsibility to reach out and impact a global world using our "staff."

Pesach gives us spiritual empowerment to succeed beyond our wildest dreams and prepare ourselves and the entire world for redemption with the speedy arrival of our righteous Moshiach. (Michtav Klali)

The Journey to Freedom starts by showing Hashem, WE ARE READY!

Belt: How can you add joy in a Mitzvah, refine your character and grow?

_____

_____

Shoes: Step up! Who needs help in your immediate environment?

_____

_____

Staff: What are your tools to reach out and impact the world?

_____

_____

Wear with pride!

(Based on Haggadah Shel Pesach Im Likkutei Taamim, Minhagim U'Biurim, Vol. II, pp. 775-784.)

Four Cups of Freedom

When promising to deliver the Jews from Egyptian slavery, G-d used four terms to describe the redemption. *(Shemos 6:6-8)*

The first three represent redemption from physical pain:

The fourth expression represents a spiritual redemption.

The four cups of wine also symbolize our freedom from four exiles:

The Egyptian, Babylonian, and Greek exiles, and our current exile, which we hope to end very soon with the coming of Moshiach.

FOUR CUPS - FOUR MOTHERS

According to Rabbi Yeshaya Halevi Horowitz, the four cups of wine we drink at the Seder symbolize the Redemptions from our four Exiles in the Merit of our four Matriarchs, Sarah, Rivka, Rochel and Leah. From them, we learn four keys to unlock the gates to redemption and create a better world.

1. The first cup used for the Kiddush, where we thank Hashem for separating us from the nations to serve Him. This corresponds to **Sarah,** who taught many women to believe in and serve Hashem.

Key to Redemption: Believe in Hashem and teach others about Hashem.

Apply: How can you strengthen your belief in Hashem? How can you inspire others to believe in Hashem?

2. The second cup is poured as we begin the Magid section of the Haggadah, recounting our origins among idol worshippers and our father Yaakov's struggle with people like Lavan. This corresponds to Rivka, who came from Lavan's household yet left idol worship and was called a "rose amongst thorns."

Key to Redemption: You are not limited by your past.

Apply: Which negative thought or habit can you change that you learned from your childhood?

3. The third cup with which we thank Hashem for our meal corresponds to **Rochel,** whose firstborn son Yosef sustained us in the time of famine.

Key to Redemption: Recognize how Hashem sustains you and sends His messengers to help you.

Apply: Express detailed recognition of Hashem and His helpers in your life.

4. The fourth cup, over which we recite Hallel, the Psalms of praise and thanksgiving to Hashem, corresponds to **Leah,** who said at Yehuda's birth, "Now I shall give thanks to Hashem." The last part of the Hallel also symbolizes our final Redemption through Moshiach, who descends from Yehuda.

Key to Redemption: Gratitude brings Redemption.

Apply: Thank Hashem each day for your blessings. How many times a day do you thank Hashem?

The Bread of Affliction

הָא לַחְמָא עַנְיָא דִּי אֲכָלוּ אַבְהָתָנָא בְּאַרְעָא דְמִצְרָיִם
כָּל דִכְפִין יֵיתֵי וְיֵיכֹל, כָּל דִצְרִיךְ יֵיתֵי וְיִפְסַח.

This [matzah] is the bread of affliction that our ancestors ate in the land of Egypt. Whoever is hungry, let him come and eat! Whoever is needy, let him come and celebrate Pesach!

We have the courage and faith of our ancestors to leave our Egypt.

What was the "affliction" that your ancestors faced in order to transmit the freedom you have today? How does their "affliction" help you see your life through a lens of gratitude? Share their stories and inspire others.

_____

_____

_____

_____

הָשַׁתָּא הָכָא, לְשָׁנָה הַבָּאָה בְּאַרְעָא דְיִשְׂרָאֵל.
הָשַׁתָּא עַבְדֵי, לְשָׁנָה הַבָּאָה בְּנֵי חוֹרִין.

Now, we are here; next year we will be in the Land of Israel…
Now, we are slaves; next year we will be FREE…

Apply the above to your physical, mental, emotional, or spiritual state. Describe your situation, emotions, sensations… Now I am/we are here…

_____

_____

By next year I/we will be free to… (Where do you see your growth?)

_____

May we all have the strength to leave our personal Egypt!

Painting by Ron Sohn

Ma Nishtana

The unique traditions at the Seder are in order to awaken the child's curiosity. Questions are asked even when no child is physically present because at the Seder, we are also addressing the child within each of us. The strong adult self speaks to the inner child with words of truth and trust in Hashem.

Take the time to answer your inner child's questions and remember that you are forever the child of Hashem, a loving and benevolent Father.

MY FOUR QUESTIONS

We relive our slavery and Exodus from Egypt.

Inspired by the Four Questions on the Seder night, reflect on these four self-discovery questions to continue your journey of transformation from personal exile to redemption.

מַה נִּשְׁתַּנָּה הַלַּיְלָה הַזֶּה מִכָּל הַלֵּילוֹת?

What makes this night different from all other nights?

Consider a challenge you experience(d), which is compared to night. Write it down. Why is this one different from other challenges? Why is it important?

___

___

1. שֶׁבְּכָל הַלֵּילוֹת אֵין אָנוּ מַטְבִּילִין אֲפִילוּ פַּעַם אֶחָת – הַלַּיְלָה הַזֶּה שְׁתֵּי פְעָמִים.

On all nights we need not dip even once, and on this night we dip twice (into the salt water and Charoset).

Why does this challenge cause your tears to flow, symbolized by the saltwater? It's ok to cry. Can you use your tears to heal, to pray from your heart and break through your limitations to discover growth?

___

___

2. שֶׁבְּכָל הַלֵּילוֹת אָנוּ אוֹכְלִין חָמֵץ וּמַצָּה, הַלַּיְלָה הַזֶּה – כֻּלּוֹ מַצָּה.

On all nights we eat leavened bread or matzah, and on this night, only matzah.

Chometz is puffed up and symbolizes ego. Matzah is flat and represents humility. It takes humility to recognize where you need to grow. How can you eliminate Chometz (ego) and only eat matzah (humility) in order to leave your personal Egypt?

3. שֶׁבְּכָל הַלֵּילוֹת אָנוּ אוֹכְלִין שְׁאָר יְרָקוֹת – הַלַּיְלָה הַזֶּה (כֻּלּוֹ) מָרוֹר.

On all nights we eat various vegetables, and on this night, bitter herbs.

Why must we face and embrace bitterness if it is more comfortable to avoid pain? Can you accept the bitter moments in life as part of Hashem's master plan? Can you reach out for support to process the pain? How can you sweeten the pain?

4. שֶׁבְּכָל הַלֵּילוֹת אָנוּ אוֹכְלִין בֵּין יוֹשְׁבִין וּבֵין מְסֻבִּין – הַלַּיְלָה הַזֶּה כֻּלָּנוּ מְסֻבִּין.

On all nights we eat sitting upright or reclining, and on this night, we all recline.

Can we act liberated even if we are still not free from this exile? How can you express gratitude and freedom NOW, even when life isn't all you want it to be?

Avadim Hayinu

THE ANSWER TO THE FOUR QUESTIONS:

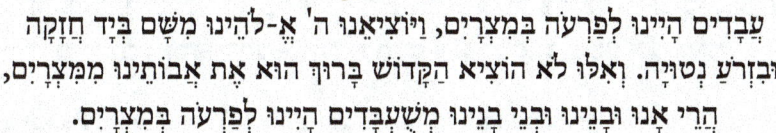

עֲבָדִים הָיִינוּ לְפַרְעֹה בְּמִצְרָיִם, וַיּוֹצִיאֵנוּ ה' אֱ-לֹהֵינוּ מִשָּׁם בְּיָד חֲזָקָה וּבִזְרֹעַ נְטוּיָה. וְאִלּוּ לֹא הוֹצִיא הַקָּדוֹשׁ בָּרוּךְ הוּא אֶת אֲבוֹתֵינוּ מִמִּצְרַיִם, הֲרֵי אָנוּ וּבָנֵינוּ וּבְנֵי בָנֵינוּ מְשֻׁעְבָּדִים הָיִינוּ לְפַרְעֹה בְּמִצְרָיִם.

We were slaves to Pharaoh in the land of Egypt. And the L-rd, our G-d, took us out from there with a strong hand and an outstretched forearm. And if the Holy One, blessed be He, had not taken our ancestors from Egypt, behold we and our children and our children's children would be enslaved to Pharaoh in Egypt.

"We were slaves in Egypt, but Hashem, our G-d, took us out."

How do these words empower you to continue to take the steps to leave your personal Egypt?

_____

_____

"If Hashem had not redeemed our ancestors, then we, our children, and our children's children would still be enslaved to Pharaoh in Egypt."

How does redeeming yourself from your personal Egypt impact others? What can you do today to heal, secure freedom or preserve Judaism for future generations?

_____

_____

It Once Happened

מַעֲשֶׂה בְּרַבִּי אֱלִיעֶזֶר וְרַבִּי יְהוֹשֻׁעַ וְרַבִּי אֶלְעָזָר בֶּן־עֲזַרְיָה וְרַבִּי עֲקִיבָא וְרַבִּי טַרְפוֹן שֶׁהָיוּ מְסֻבִּין בִּבְנֵי־בְרַק וְהָיוּ מְסַפְּרִים בִּיצִיאַת מִצְרַיִם כָּל־אוֹתוֹ הַלַּיְלָה, עַד שֶׁבָּאוּ תַלְמִידֵיהֶם וְאָמְרוּ לָהֶם רַבּוֹתֵינוּ הִגִּיעַ זְמַן קְרִיאַת שְׁמַע שֶׁל שַׁחֲרִית.

"It once happened on Pesach that Rabbi Eliezer, Rabbi Yehoshuah, Rabbi Elazar ben Azaryah, Rabbi Akivah and Rabbi Tarfon were reclining at a Seder in Bnei Brak. They were discussing the Exodus from Egypt that entire night, until their students came and said to them, "Teachers! The time has come for reciting the morning Shema!"

It is a mitzvah to tell the story of our Exodus from Egypt to our children at the Seder. Similarly, sharing personal stories of overcoming adversity empowers others to believe in the oneness of Hashem and transform their night (darkness and difficulties) into day (light and clarity). Then, they will realize it is time to declare their own Shema.

STEP INTO YOUR STORY

How does telling the story of the Exodus inspire you? How does sharing your own story open up new doors to impact yourself and others?

Step into your story. Share a story about how you or a family member overcame a personal Egypt.

The struggle (*Tzarah*), the Egypt:

What wisdom or life lessons did you gain from the journey? Who are you today because of the challenge?

The light (*Tzohar*), the Exodus:

May we join together with the ultimate redemption, when all night will turn into day and the whole world will proclaim, "Hashem is One!"

SHEMA MEDITATION

הִגִּיעַ זְמַן קְרִיאַת שְׁמַע שֶׁל שַׁחֲרִית

Each time you recite the Shema,
you are leaving Egypt again.

שְׁמַע יִשְׂרָאֵל ה' אֱ-לֹהֵינוּ ה' אֶחָד

Hear, O Israel, the L-rd is our G-d, the L-rd is One.

I take a moment to listen. To notice those moments that seem so separate from Hashem. Those feelings that seem so conflicting. Allow them to be, and feel them as they are. If they are truly from Hashem, it is all equal, there is no reason to fear. They are the gifts that are wrapped and concealed.

I look inward and find the essential truth behind the situation. Accept the oneness of Hashem in all areas of my life. The places beyond my understanding, the parts of me that seem so fragmented.

בָּרוּךְ שֵׁם כְּבוֹד מַלְכוּתוֹ לְעוֹלָם וָעֶד

Blessed be the name of the glory of His kingdom forever and ever.

Hashem is a partner in every step of this journey. He is in the sunrise and sunset, the missed opportunities and waiting places. The birds that chirp and in all my inner noise. I recognize Hashem in all the details of my life.

וְאָהַבְתָּ אֵת ה' אֱ-לֹהֶיךָ בְּכָל לְבָבְךָ וּבְכָל נַפְשְׁךָ וּבְכָל מְאֹדֶךָ

**You shall love the L-rd your G-d with all your heart,
with all your soul, and with all your might.**

I love Hashem with all my heart, all my soul and all my possessions, all that I am. There is no inner conflict, no fear. My mind and heart are one, open to receive Hashem's love. I am part of His oneness.

וְנָתַתִּי מְטַר אַרְצְכֶם בְּעִתּוֹ יוֹרֶה וּמַלְקוֹשׁ וְאָסַפְתָּ דְגָנֶךָ וְתִירֹשְׁךָ וְיִצְהָרֶךָ

I will give the rain of your land in its season, the first rains and the last rains, so that you can gather in your grain, your wine, and your oil.

Like the sprouting of a seed, my heart is sprouting love of Hashem. The seeds implanted in my mind and thoughts sprout healthy emotions.

אֲנִי ה' אֱ-לֹהֵיכֶם אֲשֶׁר הוֹצֵאתִי אֶתְכֶם מֵאֶרֶץ מִצְרַיִם

I am G-d, Who took you out of the land of Egypt.

I am FREE to break through all obstacles with Hashem's help and love today.

אֱמֶת - True

I am free to be my TRUE self and spread TRUTH!

Repeat twice a day!

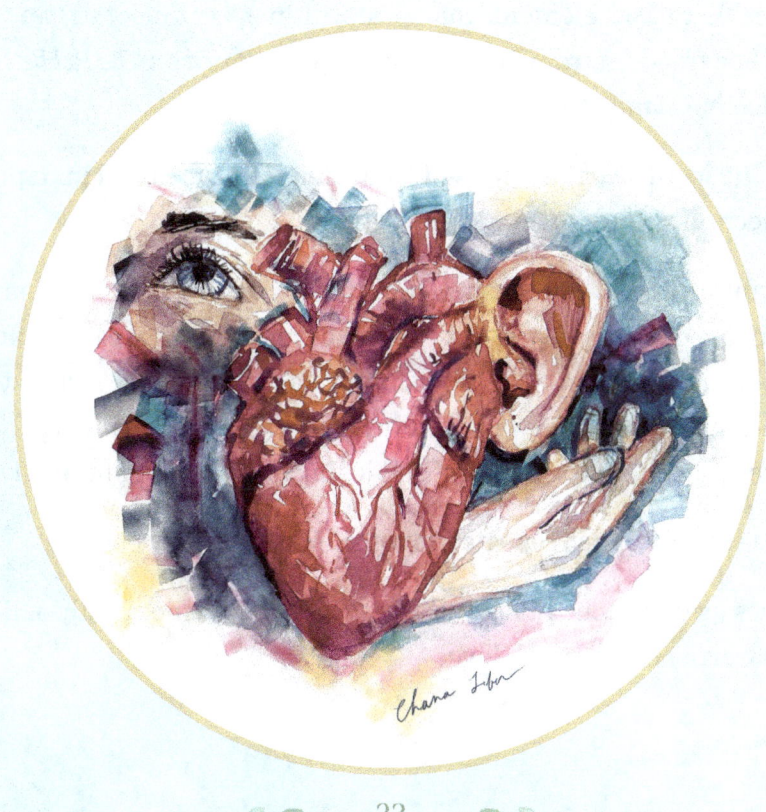

The Four Children

בָּרוּךְ הַמָּקוֹם, בָּרוּךְ הוּא, בָּרוּךְ שֶׁנָּתַן תּוֹרָה לְעַמּוֹ יִשְׂרָאֵל, בָּרוּךְ הוּא. כְּנֶגֶד אַרְבָּעָה בָנִים דִּבְּרָה תוֹרָה: אֶחָד חָכָם, וְאֶחָד רָשָׁע, וְאֶחָד תָּם, וְאֶחָד שֶׁאֵינוֹ יוֹדֵעַ לִשְׁאוֹל.

Blessed is the Omnipresent, blessed be He! Blessed is He Who gave the Torah to His people Israel, blessed be He! The Torah speaks of four children: one who is wise, one who is evil, one who is simple, and one who doesn't know how to ask.

We invite the four types of children to the Seder and since the Torah addresses all of Israel, we must say that we possess all of these "four children" within ourselves. When we accept the wise, cynical, simple, and "unable-to-ask" elements that exist within every one of us, we experience freedom from our personal Egypt. *(Based on The Rebbe's Haggadah by Chaim Miller)*

Why is the word "*baruch* - blessed" repeated four times and juxtaposed to the section about the four sons?

This reminds us that every experience in our lives is a blessing from Hashem, for our benefit. We honor and accept all four types of children that exist within. When we learn from the past, accept and embrace every part of who we are, we are truly free. Accepting and loving ourselves is the path to accepting and loving others unconditionally.

Why is the word "One" repeated to introduce each son?

It teaches us that each child has the spark of One Hashem within. Each child is worthy of Hashem's love.

Describe what you see when you visualize the spark of Hashem in yourself or another.

HEALING MY INNER CHILD

After listing the four different sons, the Haggadah continues, מָה הוּא אוֹמֵר "What does he [the son] say?" This can also be translated as, ?מָה הוּא אוֹמֵר - "What is he? [What] he says."

We can tell who a person is from their words. So, take notice of your thoughts and speech.

How and when did/does your (inner) child express these parts in the past or the present? What can you say to your (inner) child?

חָכָם מָה הוּא אוֹמֵר
WISE - Asks many questions

רָשָׁע מָה הוּא אוֹמֵר
NEGATIVE/CYNICAL - Feels Excluded

תָּם מָה הוּא אוֹמֵר
SIMPLE/SINCERE - Ignorant

וְשֶׁאֵינוֹ יוֹדֵעַ לִשְׁאוֹל
SILENT/MISUNDERSTOOD - Unable to Ask

Each child needs a different message to connect to Hashem.

1. To the Wise Child: "Your questions matter!" Answer all questions and respond to a child's curiosity.

2. To the Negative/Cynical Child: "You have a G-dly soul! You belong and will be redeemed." In addition to answering the questions, address the unspoken issues bothering the child.

3. To the Simple/Sincere Child: "Hashem took us out with a strong hand!" Share the joy of Judaism and show the child Hashem's love.

4. To the Silent/Misunderstood Child: "Let's talk. Let me tell you a story." Take initiative by opening the child to think, analyze and question.

(Based on an essay by Rabbi Naftali Silberberg for Chabad.org.)

What would it be like to accept every part of your (inner) child with total self-compassion?

From a place of self-acceptance, we heal, grow and thrive!

MEDITATION

Breathe in Hashem's love.

Exhale any negative feelings, such as fear or resentment.

HASHEM LOVES ME AS HIS ONLY CHILD.

Hashem charged Moshe, "And you shall say to Pharaoh: 'So said Hashem, "My firstborn son is Israel" (Shemos 4:22).

I am protected in the house of Hashem.

Hashem loves me!

I am Hashem's precious child.

Every part of me is welcome in Hashem's home.

I am His masterpiece.

I have something so vital to add to this world.

Hashem loves me unconditionally!

When you lose faith because you see no end,

Express your inner child and pretend.

Trust that Hashem can do anything,

Pray and sing to the King of all kings.

Live in the moment, don't worry or fret;

Trust that all your needs are being met.

Find a picture of yourself as a child. Look into the picture.
Write your inner child a letter. Instill words of hope and trust.
Help your inner child feel Hashem's unconditional love and protection.

Pick one act of kindness and tell your inner child, "I'm doing this for you because you are loved."

What will you do?

"Hashem created bitter and sweet, dark and light. I can take bitterness and turn it sweet, darkness and make it shine. I can create my own life. It will be hard, very hard. But it will be my own light. When it comes time to return it to its Creator, I will say, "Look what I made with the stuff you gave me!" And He will say, "That's my child!" *(Tzvi Freeman, Chabad.org)*

Letter from the Lubavitcher Rebbe, 11 Nissan, 5717- 1956:

"Our ancestors in Egypt were a minority and lived in the most difficult circumstances. Yet, they preserved their identity and with pride tenaciously clung to their way of life. This assured their existence and their true deliverance from slavery, physical and spiritual.

"There is no room for hopelessness in Jewish life and no Jew should ever be given up as a lost cause. Through the proper compassionate approach, even those of the lost generation can be brought back to the love of G-d and love of Torah, and not only be included in the community of the "Four Sons," but in due course be elevated to the rank of the wise son."

No Jew is ever lost. How can you physically, emotionally or spiritually uplift yourself (or another Jew) to love Hashem?

_____

_____

_____

If you think it is too hard to heal, let go of limiting beliefs or a challenging past, read on…

Humble Beginnings

מִתְּחִלָּה עוֹבְדֵי עֲבוֹדָה זָרָה הָיוּ אֲבוֹתֵינוּ, וְעַכְשָׁיו קֵרְבָנוּ הַמָּקוֹם לַעֲבֹדָתוֹ, שֶׁנֶּאֱמַר: וַיֹּאמֶר יְהוֹשֻׁעַ אֶל־כָּל־הָעָם, כֹּה אָמַר ה' אֱ-לֹהֵי יִשְׂרָאֵל: בְּעֵבֶר הַנָּהָר יָשְׁבוּ אֲבוֹתֵיכֶם מֵעוֹלָם, תֶּרַח אֲבִי אַבְרָהָם וַאֲבִי נָחוֹר, וַיַּעַבְדוּ אֱ-לֹהִים אֲחֵרִים.

From the beginning, our ancestors were idol worshipers. And now, G-d has brought us close to His worship, as it is stated (*Yehoshua 24:2-4*), "Yehoshua said to the whole people, so said the L-rd, G-d of Israel, 'Over the river did your ancestors dwell from always, Terach the father of Avraham and the father of Nachor, and they worshiped other gods.

וָאֶקַּח אֶת־אֲבִיכֶם אֶת־אַבְרָהָם מֵעֵבֶר הַנָּהָר וָאוֹלֵךְ אוֹתוֹ בְּכָל־אֶרֶץ כְּנָעַן, וָאַרְבֶּה אֶת־זַרְעוֹ וָאֶתֵּן לוֹ אֶת־יִצְחָק, וָאֶתֵּן לְיִצְחָק אֶת־יַעֲקֹב וְאֶת־עֵשָׂו. וָאֶתֵּן לְעֵשָׂו אֶת־הַר שֵׂעִיר לָרֶשֶׁת אֹתוֹ, וְיַעֲקֹב וּבָנָיו יָרְדוּ מִצְרָיִם.

'But I took your father Avraham from across the River, and I led him through the whole land of Cana'an, and I multiplied his offspring... And I gave to Yitzchok, Ya'akov and Esav; and I gave to Esav, Mount Seir [in order that he] inherit it; and Yaakov and his sons went down to Egypt.'"

Think about our humble beginnings as a nation. Avraham's ancestors were idol worshipers and he still discovered and spread the truth of One G-d. Think back to your humble beginnings and the false beliefs that you acquired. Here is a tool to help you let go of false beliefs through asking four questions and turning the thought around.

FREEDOM FROM FALSE BELIEFS

On the "Belief" line below, write down a stressful belief that arose from a situation. Allow yourself to mentally revisit the specific situation. Then question the concept in writing, using the following questions. When answering the questions, close your eyes, be still, and witness what appears to you.

Negative belief: What is your belief?
E.g. "I am not creative." "If I make a mistake, I am a loser." "Hashem doesn't hear my prayers." "I am selfish".

_____

What images of the past and future do you see when you believe the thought? How does this belief still enslave you? How do you treat yourself and others when you believe the thought?

_____

_____

What emotions arise when you believe that thought? Where do you feel these feelings in your body?

_____

_____

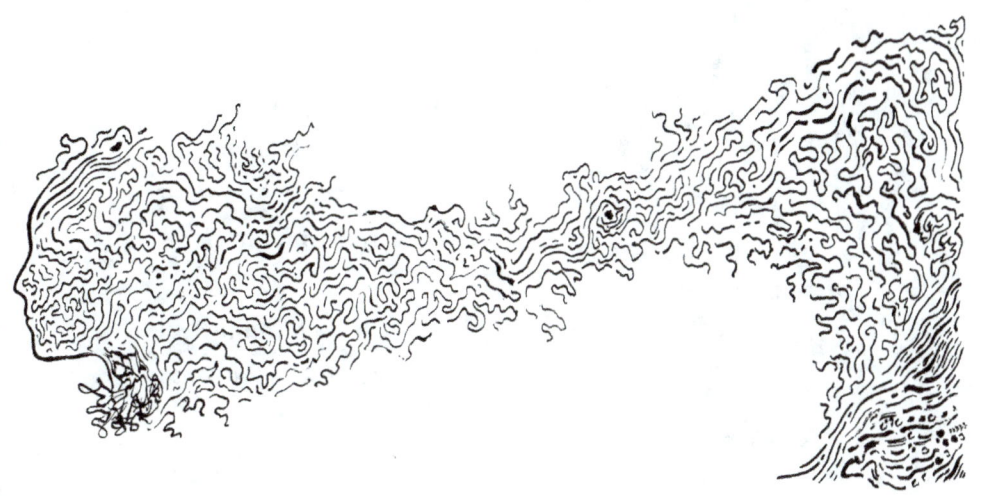

FREE TO HAVE POSITIVE BELIEFS

Positive Belief: What is the opposite of that negative thought? Reframe this false belief into a new, positive belief and open the channels for blessings in your life (like "Hashem multiplied Avraham's offspring").

_____

_____

Close your eyes and see yourself free from the negative thought. Who would you be WITHOUT the thought? What emotions arise when you believe the positive thought? Where do you feel these feelings in your body?

_____

_____

(Based on "The Work" — A Written Meditation by Byron Katie. TheWork.com)

static energy
from motion to stillness
from order to chaos

even change
can't stay the same

this land of Egypt
wraps around my being
pulled by inertia

how far it reaches
I couldn't possibly imagine

it's an Illusion of safety
life moves with entropy
inanimate static

the force is strong
the world locked within

to break this inertia
i need all my might
with help from above

to create beauty from chaos
is the art of freedom.

-Chana Laber

The Promise

בָּרוּךְ שׁוֹמֵר הַבְטָחָתוֹ לְיִשְׂרָאֵל, בָּרוּךְ הוּא. שֶׁהַקָּדוֹשׁ בָּרוּךְ הוּא חִשַּׁב אֶת־הַקֵּץ, לַעֲשׂוֹת כְּמוֹ שֶׁאָמַר לְאַבְרָהָם אָבִינוּ בִּבְרִית בֵּין הַבְּתָרִים, שֶׁנֶּאֱמַר: וַיֹּאמֶר לְאַבְרָם, יָדֹעַ תֵּדַע כִּי־גֵר יִהְיֶה זַרְעֲךָ בְּאֶרֶץ לֹא לָהֶם, וַעֲבָדוּם וְעִנּוּ אֹתָם אַרְבַּע מֵאוֹת שָׁנָה. וְגַם אֶת־הַגּוֹי אֲשֶׁר יַעֲבֹדוּ דָּן אָנֹכִי וְאַחֲרֵי־כֵן יֵצְאוּ בִּרְכֻשׁ גָּדוֹל.

Blessed be the One Who keeps His promise to Israel, blessed be He; since the Holy One, blessed be He, calculated the end [of the exile,] to do as He said to Avraham, our father, in the Covenant between the Pieces, as it is stated (*Bereishis 15:13-14*), "And He said to Avram, 'You should surely know that your seed will be a stranger in a land that is not theirs, and they will enslave them and afflict them four hundred years. And also that nation for which they shall toil will I judge, and afterwards they will go out with much wealth.'"

"He calculated the end…"

"When is the end of our current exile? Rav said: 'All the ends have passed. Now the matter depends solely on returning to G-d'" *(Talmud, Sanhedrin)*.

What is your next step towards strengthening your connection with Hashem? Share it with another for accountability.

_____

_____

_____

Our Strength

וְהִיא שֶׁעָמְדָה לַאֲבוֹתֵינוּ וְלָנוּ. שֶׁלֹּא אֶחָד בִּלְבָד עָמַד עָלֵינוּ לְכַלּוֹתֵנוּ, אֶלָּא שֶׁבְּכָל דּוֹר וָדוֹר עוֹמְדִים עָלֵינוּ לְכַלּוֹתֵנוּ, וְהַקָּדוֹשׁ בָּרוּךְ הוּא מַצִּילֵנוּ מִיָּדָם.

"And it is THIS (וְהִיא) that has stood by our fathers and us: For not just one alone has risen against us to destroy us, but in each generation they rise against us to destroy us - and the Holy, Blessed be He, saves us from their hand."

וְהִיא

The numerical value of the letters of וְהִיא hint to what "THIS" is that has stood by our fathers in each generation:

ו Vov = 6, for the Six Orders of the Mishna

ה Hay = 5, for the Five Books of Moses

י Yud = 10, for the Ten Commandments

א Alef = 1, for One Hashem

Who is your source of strength to rise above the challenges? What are your external and internal resources from Hashem that fortify you in the face of your "enemy"? (The enemy, the Voice of Pharaoh that holds you back, can be internal or external.)

Go Out and Learn

צֵא וּלְמַד מַה בִּקֵּשׁ לָבָן הָאֲרַמִּי לַעֲשׂוֹת לְיַעֲקֹב אָבִינוּ: שֶׁפַּרְעֹה לֹא גָזַר אֶלָּא עַל הַזְּכָרִים, וְלָבָן בִּקֵּשׁ לַעֲקֹר אֶת־הַכֹּל. שֶׁנֶּאֱמַר: אֲרַמִּי אֹבֵד אָבִי, וַיֵּרֶד מִצְרַיְמָה וַיָּגָר שָׁם בִּמְתֵי מְעָט, וַיְהִי שָׁם לְגוֹי גָּדוֹל, עָצוּם וָרָב.

"Go out and learn what Lavan, the Aramean, wanted to do to our father Yaakov. Pharaoh only decreed against the males, but Lavan wanted to eliminate everyone. As it is stated (Devarim 26:5), "An Aramean was destroying my father and he went down to Egypt, and he resided there with a small number and there he became a nation, great, powerful and numerous."

Why does it say, "Go out and learn"?

If you want to learn and be open to new ideas, you need to "go out" of your limited viewpoint of life. *(The Rebbe's Haggadah, by Chaim Miller)*

How can you "go out" of a limited viewpoint to receive new wisdom or insight?

Lavan and Pharaoh tried to harm Yaakov but they did not succeed.

Your "waist is belted" with the tools you need to ensure that the inner Lavan and Pharaoh don't wield their power over you. How will you use your internal or external resources (see above question) to withstand their advances? Which tool will you use today?

REFRAME

Reframing is seeing your current situation from a new, positive, G-dly perspective. It is helpful in problem solving, decision making and living with a growth mindset.

Find quiet, and listen: What is your inner "Voice of Pharaoh," a negative thought about your situation or self-talk that holds you back from taking the next step in your growth and productivity?

Reframe the thought into a positive statement.

How will your new, positive mindset have an impact on your actions? Who will you become?

Living in the world yet beyond—

Going out of Egypt reflects our personal process to leave our limitations and boundaries.

Chassidus shows us how to free ourselves from the limits and boundaries of this physical world.

Not by abandoning it, but refining and transforming it.

Perceiving the truth, that the world is in fact good, this is what Hashem willed.

Living in the world, yet beyond.

— Hayom Yom 25th Tevet

Feeling Down?

YERIDAH L'TZORECH ALIYA: WE GO DOWN TO RISE UP!

בִּמְתֵי מְעָט. כְּמָה שֶׁנֶּאֱמַר: בְּשִׁבְעִים נֶפֶשׁ יָרְדוּ אֲבוֹתֶיךָ מִצְרָיְמָה, וְעַתָּה שָׂמְךָ ה' אֱ-לֹהֶיךָ כְּכוֹכְבֵי הַשָּׁמַיִם לָרֹב.

"'Few in number' - With seventy souls your fathers went down to Egypt, but now Hashem, your G-d, has made you as numerous as the stars of the heavens" (*Devarim 10:22*).

Just like the Jews went down to Egypt in order to ultimately become the Jewish nation and receive the Torah, in life we sometimes take a fall in order to rise.

How can a low in life be a catalyst for an opportunity to grow and reach a new high?

_____

_____

_____

_____

בְּשִׁבְעִים נֶפֶשׁ - "They were seventy souls"

The Torah lists only sixty-nine names. The seventy souls were completed by the birth of Yocheved before they entered Egypt. The Rebbe teaches that the way to go out of Egypt is through being a Yocheved and using the feminine approach. It is no wonder that she mothered Moshe, who led us out of Egypt. This is accomplished when we embrace people the way they are. We nurture. We inspire. We acknowledge. We encourage others to come to an awareness of the truth by themselves. We support their efforts to become better people. *(The Lubavitcher Rebbe, Likutei Sichos, Volume 20)*

How can you grow and support yourself (or others) using the feminine, nurturing approach?

Be Fruitful

וַיְהִי שָׁם לְגוֹי. מְלַמֵּד שֶׁהָיוּ יִשְׂרָאֵל מְצֻיָּנִים שָׁם. גָּדוֹל עָצוּם – כְּמָה שֶׁנֶּאֱמַר: וּבְנֵי יִשְׂרָאֵל פָּרוּ וַיִּשְׁרְצוּ וַיִּרְבּוּ וַיַּעַצְמוּ בִּמְאֹד מְאֹד, וַתִּמָּלֵא הָאָרֶץ אֹתָם.

"And the Children of Israel were fruitful and swarmed and increased and became very, very strong, and the land of Egypt became filled with them" (*Shemos 1:7*).

How did the people swarm? "The Egyptians treated us badly, they made us suffer, and they imposed hard labor upon us" (*Devarim 26:6*). Proportionate to the oppression, the women had more children—sextuplets! In response, the Egyptians made plans to decrease the growth: "Come let us act cunningly with them, lest they increase" (*Shemos 1:10*).

How can the above detail be relevant in our day if we are not having sextuplets?

The Rebbe teaches that to leave our Egypt today, each of us should seek to have an abundance of spiritual children. The first Lubavitcher Rebbe, Rabbi Schneur Zalman of Liadi, teaches that "to be fruitful and multiply" means to give birth to another Jew by bringing him or her closer to Hashem. In this way, one emulates Miriam and the women, who did not despair at Pharaoh's harsh decrees but faithfully raised a generation of proud Jews who believed in Hashem and Moshe. *(The Rebbe's Haggadah by Chaim Miller)*

The soul of Miriam has been divided into many different sparks and one lies within YOU! Imbued with her hope in the future, it is up to YOU to bring personal redemption for yourself and for the children of our world.

In what way are you a Miriam today?

What can you do to ensure the preservation of our heritage from generation to generation? How can you get more involved in strengthening Jewish education in your home or in the world?

Pain & Prayer

וַנִּצְעַק אֶל ה' אֱ-לֹהֵי אֲבֹתֵינוּ, וַיִּשְׁמַע ה' אֶת־קֹלֵנוּ, וַיַּרְא אֶת־עָנְיֵנוּ וְאֶת עֲמָלֵנוּ וְאֶת לַחֲצֵנוּ.

"And we cried out to Hashem, the G-d of our fathers, and Hashem heard our voice and saw our affliction, our toil and our oppression (*Devarim 26:7*)...

וַתַּעַל שַׁוְעָתָם אֶל־הָאֱלֹהִים מִן־הָעֲבֹדָה.

And their prayers, prompted by the hard work, rose up to G-d" (*Shemos 2:23*).

What triggers your tears? How can you turn your tears into triumph?

When you feel like crying, let the tears flow, and listen. Listen closely to your inner voice. Is this your soul crying for spirituality, love, connection to Hashem and to others? Use the tears to reflect deeply, and turn your tears into growth. Water your garden through prayer, a good deed and a renewed deeper connection with Hashem.

Why were the Children of Israel's prayers so crucial to bringing about the Exodus from Egypt?

Rabbeinu Bechaye says: Even though the time had come for redemption, the people did not deserve it. When they cried out because of the hard work, Hashem accepted their prayers. This is a hint to our future redemption, which also depends on Teshuvah and prayer.

Remember that Hashem feels your pain. Embrace all feelings, validate your pain and turn it into a prayer. Our tears and prayers will bring an end to this dark exile.

Write a letter to Hashem. My Personal Prayer:

THE TEARS WE SHED ARE THE ONES THAT HEAL US

וַיִּשְׁמַע ה' אֶת קֹלֵנוּ. כְּמָה שֶׁנֶּאֱמַר: וַיִּשְׁמַע אֱ-לֹהִים אֶת-נַאֲקָתָם, וַיִּזְכֹּר אֱ-לֹהִים אֶת-בְּרִיתוֹ אֶת-אַבְרָהָם, אֶת-יִצְחָק וְאֶת-יַעֲקֹב.

"And G-d heard our voice" - as it is stated (*Shemos 2:24*): "And G-d heard their groans and G-d remembered His covenant with Avraham and with Yitzchok and with Yaakov."

A time when Hashem heard your voice and answered your prayers:

_____

_____

Pharaoh's decrees became harsher. The situation in Egypt worsened before it improved. It's the darkest time of night before the dawn of a new day.

What is the lesson for life?

_____

וְאֶת־עֲמָלֵנוּ. אֵלּוּ הַבָּנִים. כְּמָה שֶׁנֶּאֱמַר:
כָּל־הַבֵּן הַיִּלּוֹד הַיְאֹרָה תַּשְׁלִיכֻהוּ וְכָל־הַבַּת תְּחַיּוּן.

"And [G-d witnessed] our toil" - This is the sons, as it is stated (*Shemos 1:24*): "Every boy that is born, throw him into the Nile and every girl you shall keep alive."

Why does it say, "Every girl you shall keep alive"?

The Lubavitcher Rebbe explains that Pharaoh wanted to drown the boys physically and the girls spiritually by assimilating them into Egyptian culture.

What do you find challenging about living as a Jew today, or raising Jewish children?

_____

_____

Reflect on this question as you color in the illustration on the next page.

Miraculous Salvation

וַיּוֹצִאֵנוּ ה' מִמִּצְרַיִם בְּיָד חֲזָקָה, וּבִזְרֹעַ נְטוּיָה, וּבְמֹרָא גָּדֹל, וּבְאֹתוֹת וּבְמֹפְתִים.

"G-d brought us out of Egypt with a strong hand, with an outstretched arm, with great awe, with signs and with wonders" (*Devarim 26:8*).

Write about a time that you felt Hashem's outstretched hand and miraculous salvation:

_____

_____

Write or draw your visualization of Hashem taking you out of your personal Egypt with miracles and wonders.

Ten Plagues

אֵלּוּ עֶשֶׂר מַכּוֹת שֶׁהֵבִיא הַקָּדוֹשׁ בָּרוּךְ הוּא עַל הַמִּצְרִים בְּמִצְרַיִם, וְאֵלּוּ הֵן:
דָּם, צְפַרְדֵּעַ, כִּנִּים, עָרוֹב, דֶּבֶר, שְׁחִין, בָּרָד, אַרְבֶּה, חֹשֶׁךְ, מַכַּת בְּכוֹרוֹת.

"These are the Ten Plagues that the Holy One, blessed be He, brought upon the Egyptians in Egypt: blood, frogs, lice, wild beasts, pestilence, boils, hail, locusts, darkness, slaying of the first born."

What is the purpose of the plagues?

Were the Ten Plagues just a punishment for Pharaoh's cruelty so that he would release the Jews? If we carefully examine the Torah, we will find a deeper purpose than mere force.

When Moshe asked Pharaoh to free his people, Pharaoh responded:

"Who is Hashem that I should listen to Him and let the Jews go free? I do not know Hashem" *(Shemos 5:2)*.

Pharaoh's response hints to the purpose of the miraculous plagues, which was to make him recognize Hashem, Who stated: "[So] Egypt will know that I am Hashem" *(Shemos 7:3-5)*. Only then would Pharaoh let the Jews leave Egypt.

Not only were the plagues for Pharaoh's recognition, but for the entire Jewish people! Hashem instructed us to tell our children and grandchildren about the miracles so that they "will know that I am the Lord" *(Shemos 10:2)*.

Hashem created the world with ten utterances and continues to sustain every detail of creation with His speech. Pharaoh denied these ten Divine utterances and the Ten Plagues proved that Hashem is the all-powerful Creator.

For ancient Pharaoh, the Ten Plagues meant that he eventually acknowledged Hashem and freed the Jewish people.

For us, they mean that we recognize Hashem in the details of our lives, including every aspect of nature. Recognizing Hashem awakens our love and awe for our Creator. To do so, we take steps to connect to Him through performing Mitzvos with love and passion and avoiding unholy pursuits.

(By Tali Loewenthal reprinted with permission from chabad.org; See the Lubavitcher Rebbe's Likkutei Sichot, vol. 36, p.33)

BLOOD AND FROGS

BLOOD - PASSION
This essential of life warmed up the cold Nile.

How can you increase passion and vitality in your daily life, as the blood warmed up the cold river?

FROGS - DEDICATION
Cold-blooded frogs went against their nature to enter the fiery Egyptians ovens.

How can you break your limitations to serve Hashem with dedication, as the frogs?

Based on the Lubavitcher Rebbe's talks

EACH PLAGUE IS A STEP TO RECOGNIZE HASHEM, BRINGING US CLOSER TO REDEMPTION.

Rabbi Shmuel Hagiz explains that the Ten Plagues correspond to the various elements of nature, created by Hashem. While these aspects in nature could be explained as stable, independent forces, the plagues demonstrated that nature is dependent on Hashem.

How do you recognize your dependence on Hashem in these aspects of nature and express appreciation for Hashem's world? Fill in your answers in the third column of the chart.

	How does this Plague manifest Hashem's Kingship?	My Recognition:
BLOOD	Hashem rules over the water.	
FROGS	Hashem rules over all man-made creations (which the frogs invaded).	
LICE	Hashem rules over the dust (from which the lice emerged).	
WILD ANIMALS	Hashem rules over animals.	

PESTILENCE	Hashem rules the air we breathe (through which the disease traveled).
BOILS	Hashem rules over pain and healing.
HAIL	Hashem controls the element of fire, which rained down in the form of fire in ice.
LOCUST	Hashem rules the earth's vegetation (which the locusts attacked).
DARKNESS	Hashem rules the sky.
DEATH OF THE FIRST-BORN	Hashem rules the angels, spiritual worlds, and life and death.

Dayenu דַּיֵּנוּ

IT WOULD HAVE BEEN ENOUGH!

Dayenu is a song of gratitude. In each stanza, we recall another kindness that G-d performed for our ancestors and proclaim that it alone would have been enough of a reason to celebrate and thank Hashem.

Read through the song in English as if you just left Egypt and compose your own that relates to your life today.

כַּמָּה מַעֲלוֹת טוֹבוֹת לַמָּקוֹם עָלֵינוּ

How many are the GOOD THINGS that the A-lmighty has showered upon us!

- If He had taken us out of Egypt and not made judgments on them, [it would have been] enough for us.

- If He had made judgments on them and had not made [judgment] against their gods, [it would have been] enough for us.

- If He had made [judgment] against their gods and had not killed their firstborn, [it would have been] enough for us.

- If He had killed their firstborn and had not given us their money, [it would have been] enough for us.

- If He had given us their money and had not split the Sea for us, [it would have been] enough for us.

- If He had split the Sea for us and had not taken us through it on dry land, [it would have been] enough for us.

- If He had taken us through it on dry land and had not pushed down our enemies in [the Sea], [it would have been] enough for us.

- If He had pushed down our enemies in [the Sea] and had not supplied our needs in the wilderness for forty years, [it would have been] enough for us.

- If He had supplied our needs in the wilderness for forty years and had not fed us the manna, [it would have been] enough for us.

- If He had fed us the manna and had not given us the Shabbat, [it would have been] enough for us.

- If He had given us the Shabbat and had not brought us close to Mount Sinai, [it would have been] enough for us.

- If He had brought us close to Mount Sinai and had not given us the Torah, [it would have been] enough for us.

- If He had given us the Torah and had not brought us into the land of Israel, [it would have been] enough for us.

- If He had brought us into the land of Israel and had not built us the 'Chosen House' [the Holy Temple], [it would have been] enough for us.

MY DAYENU

When we start our prayers with expectations, or with listing what we want or lack, nothing will be "good enough." But when we start with gratitude for the basics of life, our soul and body, anything we receive afterwards is fantastic. Every detail of life becomes a celebration.

If He had _____

Dayenu, It would be enough for us... to celebrate and thank Hashem.

If He had _____

Dayenu, It would be enough for us... to celebrate and thank Hashem.

If He had

Dayenu, It would be enough for us… to celebrate and thank Hashem.

If He had

Dayenu, It would be enough for us… to celebrate and thank Hashem.

If He had

Dayenu, It would be enough for us… to celebrate and thank Hashem.

If He had

Dayenu, It would be enough for us… to celebrate and thank Hashem.

"…SPLIT THE SEA FOR US"

אִלּוּ קָרַע לָנוּ אֶת־הַיָּם וְלֹא הֶעֱבִירָנוּ בְּתוֹכוֹ בֶּחָרָבָה, דַּיֵּנוּ.

If He had split the Sea for us and had not taken us through it on dry land, [it would have been] enough for us.

Although we are no longer in Egypt, Egypt is still within us. The Jews left Egypt and faced a huge obstacle: the Reed Sea. In life, the greatest obstacles are the barriers we create in our mind. A negative feeling lasts for a few minutes, but we sustain the negativity by ruminating. Ruminating is repeatedly processing a thought or a problem without completion, and its themes are often ones of inadequacy or worthlessness. The repetition of these feelings raise anxiety, and anxiety interferes with solving the problem at hand, so then depression deepens. Chassidus teaches that thoughts are like water, always flowing. Our task is to stay afloat and not drown in a sea of negativity in our mind.

When our people stood before the Sea, they faced obstacles on all sides. The Egyptians were pursuing them from behind, there were forests with wild animals on each side, and the Sea was ahead.

When confined on the seashore, the Jews had four different reactions:

1. Let's pray. (Freeze)

2. Let's go back to Egypt. (Flight)

3. Let's drown in the sea. (Flight)

4. Let's fight. (Fight)

What is your goal? Where is your destination?

What are the obstacles surrounding your path ahead?

The 'fight-flight-freeze' or emergency response is your body's natural reaction to perceived threats; a survival instinct developed by our ancient ancestors. The reaction begins in your amygdala, a part of your brain that processes emotions. When you feel fear, the amygdala responds by sending signals to the hypothalamus, which stimulates the sympathetic nervous system and prepares your body for an emergency response.

What is your automatic reaction when you perceive danger?

In times of distress, we may react with a fight or flight or freeze in fear. Instead of feeling helpless, **listen to the voice of Moshe** and take one positive step forward and move to a better place.

Moshe encouraged the Jews at the shore: **"Stand firm [and march forward], and see Hashem's salvation!"** (*Shemos 14:13*)

Take the Plunge

One fellow named Nachshon ben Aminadav jumped into the sea and caused it to split miraculously. He was under no technical obligation to do so. However, he knew that Hashem wanted Israel to move onward to Sinai, and there was a sea in the way. So, he jumped in and plowed on toward his goal.

The Rebbe saw Nachshon's deed as a call to action: **"The lesson for all of us is to stay focused on our life's mission, disregarding all obstacles."**
(From an article by Levi Kaminker, on a talk by Lubavitcher Rebbe on Shevat 10, 5716)

What would happen if, like Nachshon, you continued marching forward, despite the obstacles, in fulfilling your higher purpose with faith that Hashem will split your sea?

What is the leap of faith - next action step - you can take on your path towards redemption?

Painting by Chanie Chanin

Visualize yourself taking the plunge. Your Sea is splitting. Watch Hashem's miracles unfold in your life. Dance with your tambourine like Miriam. Celebrate every step of your journey that has brought you to where you are today. Celebrate the people who are part of your journey in the past or present. See yourself following your path to the Mountain to receive the Torah - your G-dly mission.

Draw a picture on the tambourine of all the people in your circle of support who are dancing with you towards redemption. This may include people who are both physically alive, and those who have passed on to the next world.

The Torah

אִלּוּ קֵרְבָנוּ לִפְנֵי הַר סִינַי, וְלֹא נָתַן לָנוּ אֶת־הַתּוֹרָה. דַּיֵּנוּ.
אִלּוּ נָתַן לָנוּ אֶת־הַתּוֹרָה וְלֹא הִכְנִיסָנוּ לְאֶרֶץ יִשְׂרָאֵל, דַּיֵּנוּ.

If He had brought us close to Mount Sinai and had not given us the Torah, [it would have been] enough for us. If He had given us the Torah and had not brought us into the land of Israel, [it would have been] enough for us.

We gained freedom in order to receive the Torah and serve Hashem by observing the Mitzvot. When Hashem asked the Jews if they wanted to accept the Torah, They responded: "We will do and we will listen" *(Shemos 24:7)*!

You are chosen by Hashem to fulfill a unique mission. Your challenge is an opportunity, not a burden or punishment. Do you accept your mission?

My Mission Statement:

_____

_____

_____

_____

MEDITATION

Breathe in deeply and exhale.

*Get quiet and listen to the voice of your Divine soul within you.
It may be a whisper.*

You are not limited as long as you allow your soul to be free.

Pharaoh is no longer enslaving your mind or soul.

You recognize and accept your unique and vital mission in the world.

You have the tools to climb your mountain to serve Hashem.

You can hear the words of Hashem on your mountain.

Hashem is welcome into your heart and home.

Hashem is your partner and protector.

You live with inner calm, ease, and joy because you are never alone.

*You are connected to Hashem through Torah, Prayer, and good deeds—
the three pillars of the world.*

You are holding up the world.

You are transforming your home and the world into Hashem's home.

Breathe in deeply and exhale.

Be thankful for every breath.

*Every breath is Hashem speaking to you,
reminding you that you have a mission.*

You are needed on Earth.

Make today awesome!

Pesach, Matzah, Maror

THE MOST IMPORTANT PART OF THE SEDER

רַבָּן גַּמְלִיאֵל הָיָה אוֹמֵר: כָּל שֶׁלֹּא אָמַר שְׁלֹשָׁה דְּבָרִים אֵלּוּ בַּפֶּסַח, לֹא יָצָא יְדֵי חוֹבָתוֹ, וְאֵלּוּ הֵן: פֶּסַח, מַצָּה, וּמָרוֹר.

Rabban Gamliel used to say: "Whoever has not explained the following three things on Pesach has not fulfilled his obligation: Pesach, Matzah and Maror."

THREE KEYS TO THE SEDER - THREE KEYS TO REDEMPTION

1. PESACH - פֶּסַח

The Pesach Sacrifice that our ancestors were accustomed to eating when the Temple existed, for the sake of what [was it]? For the sake [to commemorate] that the Holy One, blessed be He, passed over the homes of our ancestors in Egypt, as it is stated *(Shemos 12:27)*; "And you shall say: 'It is the Pesach sacrifice to the Lord, for that He passed over the homes of the Children of Israel in Egypt, when He smote the Egyptians, and our homes He saved.'"

Before the Jews left Egypt, in order to merit redemption they were commanded to fulfill two mitzvot: to make the Pesach Offering, and to perform a Bris Milah. Although it was an Egyptian deity, the Jews were instructed to take a sheep, tie it to their beds, and sacrifice it after a period of inspection. With the great risk involved, this took tremendous courage and went against logic. They Jews were redeemed through aligning their will with Hashem's will.

Yes, it may take courage and self-sacrifice, but it will be worth it. How can you make Hashem's will your will for the sake of your redemption? My Pesach Sacrifice:

_____

_____

2. MATZAH - מַצָּה

This Matzah that we are eating, for the sake of what [is it]? For the sake [to commemorate] that our ancestors' dough was not yet able to rise, before the King of kings, the Holy One, blessed be He, revealed [Himself] to them and redeemed them, as it is stated (*Shemos 12:39*); "And they baked the dough which they brought out of Egypt into matzah cakes, since it did not rise; because they were expelled from Egypt, and could not delay, neither had they made for themselves provisions."

There is no time to delay. What does Hashem need from me today? My Matzah:

_____

_____

FOOD OF FAITH & HEALING

Matzah is "*michla d'mehaymnusa* - food of faith."

Why so? Because it reminds us of the faith that our ancestors had in Egypt, that they were prepared to go into a desert without any guarantees and assurances, without knowing how they'd manage to survive there, but they believed in G-d and His servant, Moshe, and that He would not forsake His Nation. And as the Prophet says, "I remember the loving kindness of your youth... your following Me in the desert" (*Yirmiyahu 2:2*). And so when a Jew eats matzah, it gives him "a shot of faith." As the Lubavitcher Rebbe says, "By simply eating matzah... this reinforces the power of faith."

And that brings us to the second thing associated with matzah: It is "*michlah d'asvasta* - food of healing." When a person has strong faith in Hashem, he'll never get spiritually ill in the first place, and as a result of that, may he not get physically ill.

We pray that by the time we sit down at our Seder table, when we eat the matzah, we'll discover within ourselves higher levels of faith in Hashem—and that faith will bring us, the Jewish Nation and the entire world healing and salvation. *(Sermon Resource for Shluchim; The Rebbe's Haggadah, pg. 34)*

A prayer, trust, or healing affirmation you can think about while eating matzah:

_____

_____

_____

3. MAROR - מָרוֹר

This Maror [bitter greens] that we are eating, for the sake of what [is it]? To commemorate that the Egyptians embittered the lives of our ancestors in Egypt, as it is stated (*Shemos 1:14*): "And they made their lives bitter with hard service, in mortar and in brick, and in all manner of service in the field; in all their service, where they made them serve with rigor."

How will you turn bitterness into bettering yourself to hasten your redemption? My Maror:

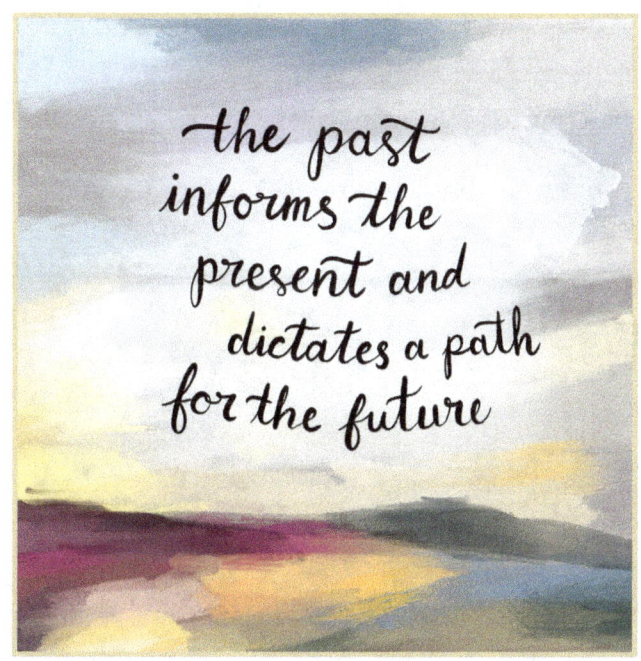

the past informs the present and dictates a path for the future

Sing & Praise Hashem

לְפִיכָךְ אֲנַחְנוּ חַיָּבִים לְהוֹדוֹת, לְהַלֵּל, לְשַׁבֵּחַ, לְפָאֵר, לְרוֹמֵם, לְהַדֵּר, לְבָרֵךְ, לְעַלֵּה וּלְקַלֵּס לְמִי שֶׁעָשָׂה לַאֲבוֹתֵינוּ וְלָנוּ אֶת־כָּל־הַנִּסִּים הָאֵלּוּ: הוֹצִיאָנוּ מֵעַבְדוּת לְחֵרוּת מִיָּגוֹן לְשִׂמְחָה, וּמֵאֵבֶל לְיוֹם טוֹב, וּמֵאֲפֵלָה לְאוֹר גָּדוֹל, וּמִשִּׁעְבּוּד לִגְאֻלָּה.

וְנֹאמַר לְפָנָיו שִׁירָה חֲדָשָׁה: הַלְלוּיָ-הּ.

Therefore, we are obligated to thank, praise, laud, glorify, exalt, lavish, bless, raise high, and acclaim He Who made all these miracles for our ancestors and for us: He brought us out from slavery to freedom, from sorrow to joy, from mourning to celebration of a festival, from darkness to great light, and from servitude to redemption.

And let us recite a new song before Him, Hallelukah!

Which of the above experiences of leaving Egypt have you experienced in your life? (Sorrow to joy, grief to celebration, darkness to light, etc.)

How can remembering those experiences help you commemorate the Exodus today?

MY NEW GRATITUDE SONG

Through gratitude, blessings flow. Below, write your song title and lyrics that express your thanks to Hashem for your personal redemption and the redemption that is yet to come.

My Song Title: _____

My Song Lyrics:

_____
_____
_____
_____
_____
_____
_____
_____
_____
_____
_____
_____
_____

We relived the slavery and redemption from Egypt and look forward to the redemption from this exile. On that day, we will sing a new song.

May we experience wonders and miracles with the coming of Moshiach now!

לשנה הבא בירושלים
Lshana Habbah B'Yerushalyim
NEXT YEAR (TOGETHER) IN JERUSALEM!

Glossary

Heb. = Hebrew | Yid. = Yiddish

Bamidbar - *Heb.* Literally, "in the wilderness"; Numbers, the fourth of the Five Books of Moses

Bereishis - *Heb.* Literally, "in the beginning"; Genesis, the first of the Five Books of Moses

Bris Milah - *Heb.* The covenant of [ritual] circumcision performed on Jewish males, usually at eight days old; the celebration marking this occasion

Cana'an - The fertile land Divinely-promised to our Forefathers, which we inherited, and it became known as the Land of Israel

Charoset - *Heb.* Literally, "clay"; a sweet, pasty mixture of fruit, nuts, and wine, symbolic of the clay our enslaved ancestors were forced to build with, into which we dip the Maror at the Seder

Chassidus - *Heb.* Literally, "piety"; Hasidism; the eighteenth-century movement based on Jewish mysticism that revived Judaism in Eastern Europe, emphasizing the power of joy, love of G-d and one's fellow, and revealing the Divine within the material world; the teachings of the movement

Chazan - *Heb.* A cantor, who leads a congregation in prayer

Chometz - *Heb.* Leaven, and leavened products in general, which are derived from grain that is allowed to ferment and rise, and are forbidden throughout Pesach

Devarim - *Heb.* Literally, "words; things"; Deuteronomy, the fifth of the Five Books of Moses

Devarim Rabbah - *Heb.* Literally, "The Great Deuteronomy"; a homiletic commentary on Devarim

Haggadah - *Heb.* Literally, "the [re]telling"; the special volume that guides the Pesach Seder, primarily recounting the Exodus narrative and the wonders G-d performed for the Jewish People

Hallel - *Heb.* Praise; a particular selection of Psalms praising and thanking G-d, typically recited during prayer-services on festivals

Hashem - *Heb.* Literally, "the Name"; G-d

K"H - *Yid.* An abbreviation of "kenahora," meaning "no evil eye," i.e. no jealousy should negatively affect one's blessings

Klal Yisroel - *Heb.* General Israel; the collective Jewish People

Korban [pl. Korbanos] - *Heb.* A sacrificial offering to G-d, from the Hebrew root meaning 'to draw close'

Kosher - *Heb.* Literally, "fit"; complying with Jewish law to be fit for a Jew's consumption, or fit to be used for ritual purposes

Likutei Sichos - *Heb.* Literally, "collected talks"; the transcribed, edited and published a collection of the Lubavitcher Rebbe's public addresses

Ma Nishtana - *Heb.* Literally, "What makes [this night] different [from all other nights?"; the introduction to the "Four Questions", usually addressed by a child who is present at the Seder

Maggid - *Heb*. Literally, "to tell"; the fifth step of the Seder in which the story of the Exodus is recounted

Maror - *Heb*. Literally, "bitter"; the bitter herbs are eaten at the Seder, invoking the bitterness of our slavery

Matzah - *Heb*. The strictly-unleavened bread that is traditionally eaten on Pesach

Mishna - *Heb*. Literally, "[to study and] review"; Rabbi Yehudah HaNasi's first compilation (circa 200 C.E.) of the orally-transmitted Torah laws; a single law from this masterwork, the basic statements of which are elucidated by the Gemara to form the Talmud

Mitzrayim - *Heb*. Egypt, from the Hebrew root meaning 'narrow straits'

Mitzvah [pl. Mitzvot] - *Heb*. Literally, "commandment"; one of the six hundred and thirteen Divine commandments in the Torah; also means "connection" from the Aramaic root of "tzavsa,"

Moshe - *Heb*. Moses

Moshiach - *Heb*. Literally, "the anointed"; the Messiah, our long-awaited Jewish leader descended from King David, who will usher in the everlasting era of Redemption, universal peace and awareness of G-d

Nachas - *Heb*. Joy and satisfaction (often in the context of parents from their children)

Nissan - *Heb*. The first Hebrew month of the Jewish (lunar) calendar; the month in which Pesach is celebrated

Pesach - *Heb*. Passover; the seven-day festival (eight outside of Israel) beginning on Nissan 15, in commemoration of our miraculous liberation from Egyptian bondage; the name of the special offering brought up in the Holy Temple on Passover Eve

Seder - *Heb*. Literally, "order"; the service observed on the first night of Pesach (the first two nights outside of Israel), which includes recounting our exodus from Egypt, praise to G-d, and a festive meal

Shema - *Heb*. Literally, to "hear"; the Biblically-mandated declaration of devotion to G-d and faith in His Oneness, recited daily in the morning and evening

Shemos - *Heb*. Literally, "names"; Exodus, the second of the Five Books of Moses

Shluchim - *Heb*. Emissaries; this expression is frequently used in reference to Chabad-Lubavitch Rabbi-and-wife teams who further Jewish life and involvement

Talmud - *Heb*. Literally, "study"; the primary compendium of Jewish law and thought, which is subdivided into tractates; while the unspecified term usually refers to the edition developed in the Babylonian Talmudic academies and revised at the end of the fifth century C.E., the Jerusalem Talmud, was also compiled in Israel at the turn of the fourth century C.E.

Teshuvah - *Heb*. Literally, "return"; repentance; return to G-d and one's own inner essence

Yerida l'Tzorech Aliya - *Heb*. "Descent for the purpose of [a greater] ascent"

Zohar - *Heb*. The classic text of Jewish mysticism, authored by the second-century sage Rabbi Shimon bar Yochai

In Loving Memory of
SHALOM HALEVI BEN SHMUEL GUREWICZ
Yahrzeit - 10 Nissan 5781

Please do a Mitzvah in honor of Shalom. Be like him today!

Selfless
Loving
Warm
Devoted
Practical
Funny
Strong
Like a rock
No drama
Even keeled
Humble
More humble
The humblest
Love learning
Interested in how to help the world
Accepting of others differences
Deeply committed to Judaism
Deeply committed to family

Written by Chaya Sarah Gurewicz

Tribute Dedication by Shoshana & Raphael Fox

Dear Chaya Sarah Shetichye,

Can a full and complete heart ever become incomplete?

 Notice how a pair of the Hebrew letters lamed, when reflecting one another, form a heart. Similarly, when two individuals seek to complete one another, faithfully corresponding and holding space for the other's celebrations and struggles, they generate what the Torah calls "*ahavah*," love, from the root-word meaning, "to give."

If I press clay into a mold of the pair of letters lamed, the heart that takes shape in the center will remain even once the mold is lifted away. The love a couple creates through sharing their lives endures beyond the body's passing and molds them forever as one whole.

At Creation, Hashem formed Adam and Chava as one being, but back-to-back, and then separated them with a challenge to face one another. Chaya Sarah, day after day you faced the *pnimius* (inwardness - like *paneem*, face) of your beloved husband with such a *pnimius halev* of your own that you are fused as one.

He supports you as you continue to dance together; he is now your shadow, or a beam of light, following you, revealing your greatness wherever you go as an *Eved Eloki*.

We also find brokenness, yet wholeness, at the Pesach Seder.

Before reciting the Haggadah, one breaks the matzah, reserving the larger portion for the afikoman. The symbolism of this ritual is twofold: Matzah is called "*lechem oni*," the bread of poverty. Breaking it invokes the Talmudic remark (*Pesachim 115b*), "The poor can afford only a morsel." Matzah also represents redemption. Reserving a portion of it demonstrates our anticipation for ultimate redemption, heralded by the Moshiach and miracles superior to those surrounding the Exodus.

The Sfas Emes adds that hiding the afikoman prior to eating it represents the obscurity of the exact date of redemption. Nevertheless, our faith in its imminent revelation enables us to withstand the present exile, or *Golus*.

The division of body and soul is a devastating event, and propels us to search for wholeness once more. In *Golus*, a time of fragmentation where Hashem is hidden, He wants us to search for Him - and for Shalom - as we beg Hashem to reunify us with Moshiach.

www.ingramcontent.com/pod-product-compliance
Lightning Source LLC
Chambersburg PA
CBHW072105290426
44110CB00014B/1829